EVERYBODY LOVES GRACE

An Amazing True Story of How Grace
Brings Love to Everyone She Meets

D1113173

This work depicts actual events in the life of the author and her dog Grace as truthfully as recollection permits. All persons within are actual individuals; there are no composite characters.

Age range: 6-10

Summary: An amazingly true story that captures the heart as it moves us from laughter to tears and teaches us to believe in the power of love. This is a story of one dog's ability to love unconditionally and maintain her courage through periods of uncertainty. It is a story that you will want to go on forever and ever.

Publication date: October 2018

ISBN Print: 978-1-948512-00-8
ISBN eBook: 978-1-948512-01-5
ISBN ePDF: 978-1-948512-02-2
Library of Congress Control Number: 2018955006

1. Dogs 2. Adventure 3. Inspirational 4. Humor 5. Love 6. Caring 7. Healing 8. Friendship
I. McQuaid, Katy. II. Everybody Loves Grace: An Amazing True Story of How Grace Brings Love to Everyone She Meets

Everybody Loves Grace may be purchased at special quantity discounts for sales promotions, community events, book clubs, animal shelters, service or therapy dog organizations, and educational purposes for churches and schools. We welcome joint ventures for dog related fund raising events. Have Katy speak at your organization or special event. For more information contact Katy at 703.531.7755 or email her at katy@everybodylovesgrace.com

Illustrator: Susan Lavalley susanlavalleyillustr8r@gmail.com
Layout and Design: Megan VanVuren
Website: www.everybodylovesgrace.com
Publishing Consultant: Mel Cohen http://inspiredauthorspress.com/
Publisher: Everybody Loves Grace Publishing
Printed in the United States of America

Everybody Loves Grace gives children of all ages wonderful strategies for moving through the major life events they will encounter. Learning to bring a hope-filled lens to life regardless of what happens is very important to creating the outcomes they desire.

Conscious Transformation Founder, Joey Klein

Everybody Loves Grace combines love, compassion and understanding in a heartwarming true story of Grace, as she interacts with people throughout her life, during some of the most challenging experiences of loss, change and uncertainty. Grace is my favorite kind of hero—she has the superpower to just look into the eyes of any person and make them feel important. Grace's story gives children the courage to face life's most difficult situations, by knowing that there is kindness in the world and things will work out for the best. This is definitely a book for your keeper shelf in your classroom or home library.

Michelle Windmueller, Ph.D.

Change is difficult, which is why uplifting stories on transition are always welcome. Grace moves through life's changes with courage and optimism underpinned with a knowing confidence that she'll be fine on the other end of the challenge. As a senior military officer, I've seen first-hand the challenges children have moving every few years and living a life filled with change. A must-read for children who experience fear or resistance to change in their lives.

Major General Stephen T. Denker, USAF (Retired)

What a delight! Following Grace on her adventures, whether they are her first plane ride leaving the farm for a city or her daily stroll around the neighborhood, shows how poignant moments are created in the midst of daily living. Grace's sharp-eyed and optimistic outlook on life is something to aspire to, no matter what your age.

Curtis W. Fentress, Principal Designer and Founder of Fentress Architects. Co-founder of Aerial Futures

Dogs are the earthly bearers of unconditional love and you see it clearly throughout the story of *Everybody Loves Grace*! Katy's and Grace's adventures are visually tangible to bring delight to all - from children and grandchildren all the way to the reading circle at school or The Humane Society. I can't wait to share this book!

Arlene Post, Vice President, Client Services at Venturion Career Management, Philanthropist

Run, don't walk, to get a copy of *Everybody Loves Grace: An Amazing True Story of How Grace Brings Love to Everyone She Meets*! This beautiful story of Grace and her owner, Katy, and their many adventures together, will capture your heart and mind. Just by looking deeply into your eyes, Grace loves and supports you with her own kindness. With so many distractions in today's world, we all often forget to just "stop" and listen to our inner voice and what's going on around us. The simple message of profound acts of kindness that Grace demonstrates, deeply penetrates each of our longings for inner peace and calm and might even transform our own work in the world.

Personally knowing Katy and Grace has made *Everybody Loves Grace* extra special for me as I follow along on their adventures together. I hope you, the reader, experience the same profound love and adventure that Grace can give you and feel inspired to give to others. And if you happen to be in Denver, and Katy and Grace are not out adventuring, you should most definitely pay them a visit and see for yourself!

Maryann Hrichak, Ethnographer, Photographer and TechWomen Mentor

DEDICATION

I dedicate this story to Tinto and Grace
for showing me the true meaning of
unconditional love.

TABLE OF CONTENTS

ACKNOWLEDGMENTS

I would like to express my sincere gratitude to the following individuals. Without their support and guidance, this book would not have been possible.

Thank you Beth Nicoson, for many years you encouraged me to write a book. You never gave up and just knew there was a story to be told; that story is now a reality and the first book in a three-book series. You also connected me to an incredible publishing consultant.

Thank you Mel Cohen, my publishing consultant. I clearly remember that first phone call when you told me I *really* had a story. I am so grateful for your guidance throughout the creation of the book and making sure every detail was covered and all the right professionals were put into place.

A heart felt thank you to Susan Lavalley. Your illustrations truly capture the essence of Grace and others in the story and your illustrations make the story very special.

X

This beautiful story was made even better with the creative graphic design of Megan Van Vuren and editing of Tracy Johnson.

I'm also very grateful for Jill Cofsky who provided the perfect voice for Grace in the audio book and does amazing work with children's literacy initiatives.

Everybody Loves Grace would never have happened without the support of great friends. Thank you Dr. Andi and Dr. Hemerson for always being there for Grace and the extraordinary care you provide for her.

Katie Mount, without your guidance and being with me every step of the way, the story wouldn't be what it is. Maryann Hrichak, I'll never forget you stepping in to help when I needed it the most.

Last, but not least, thank you Grace for being by my side throughout the creation of this book and letting me tell your story.

FOREWORD

Katy McQuaid and I met seven years ago in a tree-lined Denver neighborhood through our dogs, Tinto and Clover. Over time, they became the best of friends, as did Katy and I. Grace joined Katy and Tinto's family soon after and became part of our group. We would play in each other's homes and go for walks, admiring the historic Queen Anne style homes in our area with their stained glass windows and wrap around porches. When we had more time we would all go to the park and play fetch, our favorite game. Although Tinto and Clover have both passed on, Katy and I remain good friends and Grace has become my "god-dog."

The title of this book is amazingly suitable: Everybody *does* love Grace! And Grace *does* bring love to everyone she meets. Grace serves as a catalyst for bringing people together in our community and provides inspiration to all who meet her. Everyone cannot help but smile when Grace looks into their eyes with keen wit and genuine care. Grace welcomes adventures head-on, and she experiences such glee in the smallest, most routine activities. Grace's love is for everyone, without discrimination. Her calm presence and kind eyes can touch even the hardest heart. We can all learn so much from Grace and the perspective she has on everyday life.

This book characterizes Grace perfectly. Grace is love, a love that is strong, loyal, and unconditional. It's the kind of love that is powerful enough to break down barriers. I wish you could meet Grace in person. At least you can meet her in this book and others that will follow. Enjoy!

Agatha Kessler, Visionary, Philanthropist. Prior executive of VISA and Hewlett-Packard, Co-founder of Aerial Futures, and most importantly Katy's friend and Grace's godmother

Chapter 1

The Adventures of Grace Begin

Hello, my name is Grace and I grew up on a farm located in the beautiful and snowy mountains that were far away from the city.

There always seemed to be a buzz of activity between us dogs running and snooping around the farm and the kids who lived there.

2

The best part of the day was when one of the kids came home from school. I just couldn't wait for Jenny to come in the door. She always started petting me right away and I would roll on my side wanting her to pet my belly! That is, until we began to play fetch with a tennis ball before she began her homework.

I don't really like to talk about it, probably

because being a mother was a lot of work for me, but I should mention I had lots of puppies when I lived on the farm— twenty puppies to be exact, in two litters. The puppies were very sweet and cute, and they looked just like me, black and tan puff balls with little brown eyes!

Friends came by to see the puppies almost every day. They cuddled and kissed my babies as they were "oohing and ahhing" over how cute they were. What they didn't know is, it was a lot of work for me to take care of all those puppies. As these friends paraded through the farm, one by one all the puppies were adopted by their new families and they moved to their forever homes.

I had a Dad on the farm and he had a job not many people do; it was a scary job driving BIG BIG trucks on dangerous roads to take food and fuel to people who lived way out in the country. He wasn't home very often and when he was, he was always busy with other things.

One day Dad came home and said, "There are too many dogs on this farm and one of them has to go!"

I also had a Mom on the farm. One day I heard her talking on the phone so I wasn't surprised when she said, "Grace, it's time for you to go. You are going to a big city with lots of people." I knew big changes were coming, and I was ready! I was excited to see what city living was all about. Besides, flying on a plane for the first time would be an adventure!

Chapter 2

Grace Flies on a Plane

Mom and Jenny drove me to the airport, and I overheard them saying how much they were going to miss me. When we got to the airport, they gently placed me into a big crate. The nice people at the airport brought me water and spoke to me softly. They loaded me and my crate into the bottom of the airplane where the suitcases go. I was

afraid because this place was dark and
noisy. Wow, those plane engines were
loud, but I was so tired I fell asleep.

When I woke up, the plane landed in
Denver and I met my new Mom, whom

I decided to call Mommy. I could sense she was nervous so I didn't look at her right away. Then I did what I do with everyone I meet. I looked straight into her pretty green eyes and all the way into her heart.

Chapter 3

Grace Arrives at Her New Home

Mommy put me on a leash and walked me over to the loading dock at the top of some stairs. "It's okay Grace, just step down," Mommy said. She didn't know I'd never seen or walked down stairs in my entire life. I had to learn fast because that was the only way to get down to a dry, grassy field where I could go potty.

Yikes, did I ever need to do that after my first plane ride!

And then guess what? There was a BIG brother waiting for me at the front door when I arrived at my new home! His name was Tinto and he shared with me all of his favorite sniff spots as we walked around the neighborhood. He also made it clear that I was NOT allowed on Mommy's bed!

Soon after I settled into my new home, Mommy's friend came over to meet me. While I was playing with her, she whispered very seriously in Mommy's ear, "Grace needs a bath." Well, I have to say, I didn't get baths on the farm so

I was very surprised when I was placed into a tub full of warm, bubbly water. Soaking like this felt so comforting and the shampoo smelled just like flowers.

As I jumped out of the tub, Mommy walked toward me with a fancy looking machine in her hands that was VERY LOUD and it blew hot air that swirled

my hair dry! It felt really good to be clean and smell good after my warm bath. Mommy's friend spent the night and she kept playing with me. I think Tinto was happy too because I smelled a lot better.

I wanted to walk fast and run, but Tinto was much older than me. He couldn't walk fast anymore because of his age so I walked slower than him. This way

he could be the leader in front of me. I
knew Tinto was happy to have me as a
little sister because he smiled, wagged
his tail, and let me play with his favorite

toy, a stuffed Dalmatian. Over time, he slowed down and I don't think he was feeling very well. While Mommy was working, Tinto rested at the foot of her bed and even though I wasn't supposed to, I broke the rules and hopped up on the bed to protect him.

Chapter 4

Grace Explores New Places

One of our favorite walks was around the city block where we lived. Groups of nice people stopped us to say hello while we were walking. One man, Joe, who was eighty-four years old, came down the sidewalk in a chair with wheels on it. Mommy told me it is called a wheelchair. He did this almost every day. We usually saw him at this

one corner where there were lots of
good sniffs. He always stopped to say
hello and pet me for a long time. He
said it was always the best part of his
day when he saw Tinto and me.

Our walks got shorter as the days went
by and Tinto stopped often. One day he

just couldn't get up as he laid on his bed. I got close to him, sniffed his ears so he knew I was nearby, and brought him his favorite toy. I loved Tinto SO much; it was hard to say goodbye to him when he died. I cried! He taught me how to love no matter what.

I watched my Mommy be sad after Tinto died and knew that I could help her be happy again. Sometimes Mommy sat by the fire and read with me at her feet. Many times I asked her to take me for walks because I knew that being outside was good for her and it helped her breathe better.

Then something special happened when

it was just Mommy and me. When we started our walks Mommy would ask me, "Which way do you want to go Grace?" Gosh, no one had EVER asked me what I wanted to do! This was such a surprise. I could tell Mommy really loved me, and I knew life was going to be extra special living with her in the city.

Sometimes I would test Mommy to see if she was really going to let me choose which way we went on our walks. I did this by walking and walking and walking. Sure enough, Mommy would let me lead the way. She never seemed to get tired—no matter how long we walked!

Of course, once in a while Mommy would say, "Grace, we've got to make our walk quick this morning because I have to go to a meeting." I listened to her on those mornings. I walked fast and didn't go too far so Mommy would be on time for her meetings.

I like it when Mommy tells me how long she's going to be gone for work or a movie. This way I can be sure to be awake when she gets home. Mommy leaves early in the morning to go to the office. Sometimes she gets home a little later than usual and I figured out those are the days she goes to the gym or meets her friends after work. That's okay because she always tells me when she's going to be later than usual and it makes me happy that she is taking care of herself.

It didn't take long for Mommy to take me to all kinds of places: Trader Joe's, the coffee shop, and restaurants where we could sit outside.

When I walk down the street, I see that everyone knows my name! They say, "There's Grace…isn't she cute?" When I get called a fluff ball, which happens all the time, it doesn't upset me because everyone says it with such love in their voice.

Sometimes I make Mommy walk me down Broadway. It's a busy street with lots of people, bikes, and some people sleeping on the sidewalk. They don't have beds like Mommy. I say hello to some of the people because I can just feel they need love. Sometimes I can tell Mommy is in a hurry, but when she

hears the person say, "You just made my
day," she gets a big smile on her face
and I can feel her great love for me too.

Chapter 5

Grace Goes on Car Adventures

When Mommy and I get into the car, it means we are going someplace special. I always like to ride in the car because it means we will have an adventure together. One of my favorite car rides was to a place not very far away. When I got out of the car, there were all these delicious smells of barbecue. It turns out we were at a barbecue festival in

the mountains! There were so many people walking on the streets and sidewalks, all I could see were knees and more knees! The smell of food was so yummy. Once in a while, when Mommy wasn't looking, I would catch a piece of barbecue as it fell to the ground.

There was another time when Mommy took me for a ride in the car. It was a special day because it was just the two of us! We were going to the mountains for a hike when I started to hear drops on the roof of the car. It started to rain—drip, drip, drip. When I got up on the seat to look out the front window, I saw two things that looked like sticks

going back and forth—swish, swish, swish—they kept the front window clear so Mommy could drive safely. It was so much fun to watch the sticks go back and forth.

Every now and then Mommy takes me to one of my favorite places, a house in the mountains. I am always so happy when we go there because each time it is a new adventure. I like it because we usually stay two or three days. I can tell when we are going there because the road gets very curvy. I can always smell the pine trees as we get closer because they are a very different smell than the city.

When we get to the house in the mountains, it is very quiet and there are lots of animals in the woods nearby. I can hear the water coming down the stream by the house, and deer come to visit us often. One day as I was resting on the porch, I saw a big, black bear on the driveway. I wasn't afraid, but I wanted Mommy to know there could be danger so I started to bark. I don't usually bark but I thought this time it was important. Mommy came outside right away to be with me, and we watched the bear from a distance. Sometimes I would growl deep in my throat to let the bear know he better not come up to our house!

I can always tell when there are other animals nearby, so I stay close to the house. I like to breathe in the fresh air when I'm in the mountains. It seems like I can hear sounds that are coming from miles away. I really like being with Mommy in the mountains for quiet time together.

Chapter 6

Everybody Needs Grace

Back to living in the city. On the walk where we see Joe, there's a house on the corner with a sign on the front that says VIOLIN MAKER. I can only imagine the beautiful sounds that come from the violins made at the house, and it has some of the best sniffs in the neighborhood. Lots of dogs like it here by the fence on the busy corner, and it was also one of Tinto's favorite spots!

Right behind the Violin Maker there is a red, brick building where many precious people come in and out of the front door. They go there for help in

finding jobs or for special treatment.
There's this one boy who I see almost
every day and he always dresses in
gray pants and a sweater. He used to
be afraid of me and every time I saw
him, he would get a little closer to me. I
noticed he wouldn't look at Mommy or
anyone else who walked by.

Finally, he started to look at me and I
would look at him. It didn't take long;
he started to smile and then he would
come up and pet me. I didn't want him
to be afraid of me so I was very careful
to be extra gentle with him and not
look into his eyes for too long. I was so
happy because I knew he was special

and needed a friend, and he picked me
to be his friend.

I started to understand that almost
everybody that walks by stops
to pet me. I'm not sure why
this happens. I just look into
people's eyes and let
them pet me.
Sometimes I

give them a paw and look deeper into their eyes. The boy at the red, brick building taught me that *Everybody needs Grace.*

I know that many of these people just need to be loved. I do my best to look them in the eyes and let them know they are loved.

One of my favorite things to do is pull Mommy into Walgreens when we walk on Broadway. After I sniff around a bit, I go to the back of the store to visit people waiting in line for their medicine. Mommy says I just know when a person needs love and kindness, and I wait for their hands to start petting me. It always works!

Another fun thing I like to do is visit a big hospital that is near my house. The letters on the side of the big, red brick building say DENVER HEALTH. I like to go there in the morning when there are lots of people walking on the sidewalks. There are doctors, nurses, ambulance drivers, and patients. Some people are there visiting their sick family and friends. I can tell these medical professionals have big hearts and important jobs caring for patients. I often catch a sniff of coffee as people stop to pet me.

One day this man with shiny black
shoes, gray hair, and a gold badge on his
black sweater that said CAPTAIN was
walking in front of me and talking to a
nurse dressed in her uniform. He saw

me out the corner of his eye, quickly stopped walking, and looked straight at me. He said, "My, she is a sweet dog. I wish I could start my day like this every day." I decided to give him my paw and he petted me gently. I was happy I could spend some time with him and help brighten up his day.

We have to cross a very busy street to get to the hospital. I started to ask Mommy if we could go there by gently pulling on my leash. Mommy looked at me and said, "Grace, 6th Avenue is far too busy for us to cross in the middle of the street." So, she took me to the crosswalk. We still run across the street

because many of the cars go very fast.
I think it's because the drivers are in a
hurry to get to work.

Our house is close to the hospital, and
there are fire trucks and ambulances
with loud sirens and flashing lights
that zoom by us. The sirens are so loud
that Mommy covers her ears. I always
want to know where the trucks and
ambulances are going. I also think about
the people they are going to help and
hope they are going to be okay.

One day, I went into the old Mayan
Theater to see a movie. As soon as we
went in the door I again heard, "Oh,
there's Grace!" Mommy thinks it's a

lot of work for me to be with people, but I don't. It's what I'm here to do. If I can make one person's life easier just by looking at them—straight into their eyes—then I'm happy.

I haven't told you much about the building I live in. It's a downtown condo. There are many special things about living there. While most people think it's hard on me living in a home without a yard, it isn't. I think it's very special living at the condo. I get to see so many people and make a difference in their lives just by looking at them straight in the eye. I often hear people say, "Grace is the best dog in the

building" or "Grace is the sweetest
and gentlest dog I've ever met." I don't
know if this is really true, but I do enjoy
making people happy. It just seems so
easy!

Chapter 7

Grace Gets Special Treats

I think Tuesdays are special; I call them "Treat Tuesdays." I just know when it is Tuesday, and around 3:00 in the afternoon I ask Mommy to take me for a walk. Of course, the real reason I want to go out is because when we walk through the lobby, there's a plate full of freshly baked treats! They smell so good and taste delicious. I gently pull on my leash to get over to where the treats are, and I can usually find lots of crumbs on the floor. I try to tell Mommy that I am helping Jose, the man who cleans the floors every day.

There's a man who comes to work in the building every night when the sun goes down. His name is Joe and he wears a blue coat that says SECURITY on it. He always greets me with a warm smile and asks, "How is my Grace doing today?" I walk right over to him and he puts out his hand and asks for my paw.

I wish I could stay with Joe because when he is working security, I could be greeting all the people as they

come home for the night. He brings
in almonds as a special treat for
me. I listen to him ask Mommy for
permission on how many almonds he

can give me. He counts the almonds and I wait patiently for him as he gives them to me one by one. Once in a while, Joe runs out of almonds and he tells me, "Grace, you forgot to call me to remind me to buy more almonds." He makes me laugh because I'm sure he knows I don't have a telephone! When I'm finished eating the almonds, Joe gets up from his chair and walks me to the elevator. I think Joe loves me very much and I love him too.

Chapter 8

Grace Meets so Many Special People

We have a new neighbor at our condo that gets his vanilla coffee in the lobby every morning. He rides in a wheelchair and his name is Bobby. His wheelchair is different from Joe's. Bobby's wheelchair has a motor on it. When I see him outside, he is always driving his wheelchair very fast! It's fun to watch him smile as he zooms down the sidewalk. He always stops to say hello to me. I like to smell his coffee when he stops to pet me. I can tell Bobby is very special and he is so kind to me. I laugh when Mommy says to him, "Bobby, be careful. You drive your wheelchair like a race car driver!" Bobby just winks at me as if to say, "I'm not planning to slow down!"

I like living in the city because there are so many people. I get to meet the young, the old, babies, people who are happy, sad, fun, serious, healthy, and the sick. I'm so glad I moved here because I get to meet so many different types of people!

I learned a lot when I got to Denver, and it was just the beginning. Mommy likes to take me with her on many adventures.

I hope you will join me and Mommy on a travel adventure to The Grand Canyon in our next book. This is how the adventure started.

The best thing EVER happened just after Mommy stopped working at her job. She was sitting at her desk one day and I overheard her talking on the phone. "Really, Uncle Pete, you want me to come visit you in Arizona? How long of a drive is it? Okay, when I visit, I'll be sure to bring Grace with me!"

Just hearing the words "visit" and "drive" made me SO excited!! I knew I was going to have a fun-filled great adventure! Only a few days later, Mommy took a suitcase out of the closet. This wasn't like the other times Mommy traveled—there was something special about it. I could see a small pile started with a few of my things: my blanket, my blue travel cooler for my food, my extra water bowl, my soft, pink bone toy, and an extra-long leash for exploring.

This is going to be a GREAT adventure, I could just tell!

I could hardly sleep at night knowing we were going on a road trip soon. I was sure I was going on the trip, but just in case, I slept right next to Mommy's bed each night. Sure enough, one morning when it was very early, Mommy got out of bed and said, "Grace, today we are going on a long adventurous road trip. Will you be my co-pilot?" "Of course," I said. I know Mommy heard me. She could see how excited I was!

FINNISH LAPPHUNDS

Finnish Lapphunds were originally used to herd reindeer—yes, reindeer in Finland. Although it is one of the most popular dog breeds in its native country, Finland, it is not very numerous outside of the Nordic countries.

Finnish Lapphunds are an easy going, very intelligent, and active breed. Lappies, as they are called, are known for loving people and have a gentle nature with children, people with disabilities, and the elderly. With their love of people, they like to use their herding instincts to keep people and other pets together.

One of the things Lappies do really well is to stay focused and watch what goes on around them. They are curious and it is rare for them to miss a trick! They become members of the family immediately because they like everyone: babies, kids, parents, and other pets.

Since they are known for their skill as herders—or the ability to "round 'em up"—Lappies appreciate the opportunity to explore outside. They are perfect companions for people who like to walk, hike, mountain bike, or go camping.

Probably the most important trait of a Finnish Lapphund is to look into people's eyes and let them know they are loved.